Two Hearts
(*Poetry*)

By:
Mamatkarimova Baxriniso

© Taemeer Publications LLC
Two Hearts *(Poetry)*
by: Mamatkarimova Baxriniso
Edition: August '2023
Publisher:
Taemeer Publications LLC (Michigan, USA / Hyderabad, India)

© Taemeer Publications

Book	:	Two Hearts *(Poetry)*
Author	:	Mamatkarimova Baxriniso
Publisher	:	Taemeer Publications
Year	:	'2023
Pages	:	44
Title Design	:	*Taemeer Web Design*

Contents

1	Be kind to me	5
2	O life...!	6
3	I missed	7
4	I'm wandering	8
5	What is happening in our time?	9
6	Calling Navoi	13
7	Faithful	15
8	The future of Uzbekistan	17
9	People have changed	19
10	My phone	20
11	you don't love me	21
12	Good luck	23

13	Happy day	25
14	To the tourist	26
15	Memories	28
16	Winter	30
17	Life	31
18	Boring life	34
19	My mom	35
20	Truth	36
21	My meaningless days	38
22	Love	40
23	Depression	41

1
Be kind to me

Please don't play with my feelings

Please don't destroy my heart

My true love for you

Please appreciate it

I have no other person but you

Don't draw any other pencil than me

Balma language is different and language is different

Oh my eyes don't fill with tears

Be dear to me

Be a loyal friend like Alpomish

Be the person of my dreams

Be my support, my support, my kindness

2
O life...!

Do not suspect life from me

I love him, believe me

Jealousy is strong and bad

I love him, I miss him badly

Did I say I love you, trust me

Don't make me wander so much in love

When he looks into my eyes, his eyes are bright

We will be happy and our life will be prosperous

Have you tried so many times?

Or is love just sadness, longing and pain?

Give us happiness, love and life

We have the right to be happy, O life

3
I missed

Ask me how I am

I really miss you

Maybe you miss me too

Tell me I'm waiting

You taught yourself

You took a place in my heart

Without remembering these days

You missed it

You don't answer my calls

You don't reply to my messages

I don't know why you don't show up

Answer my questions

I missed. Just remember

Tell me, what's on your mind?

Or is it easy for you to forget me?

My love was you, man

4
I'm wandering

My crazy love

My love makes me wander

My love interest

My love bothers me

where are you my love

My love understand me

I'm happy where you are

Don't make me unhappy

Who created fate?

Alib address-place

I started the ways of life

I wander in search of happiness

I will go, I will come

I hope for happiness

Of course I know

I will be happy one day

I'm confused, I'm confused

I'm looking for happiness

I burn, I burn

I'm crazy in search of happiness

5
What is happening in our time?

There is creativity in the hijab,

I miss the time.

Girls dreams are broken

What happened to our time?

God-given beauty,

The hand of man destroys.

As if he knows

What happened to our time?

I didn't know if it was the end of time,

What happened to people?

I didn't think of the ending,

What happened to our time?

Masculine is a feminine quality,

Women know their own men.

It's all crazy,

What happened to our time?

Sometimes I think,

Don't wake up if you have a dream.

Am I oblivious or am I

What happened to our time?

What is happening in our time?

There is creativity in the hijab,

I miss the time.

Girls dreams are broken

What happened to our time?

God-given beauty,

The hand of man destroys.

As if he knows

What happened to our time?

I didn't know if it was the end of time,

What happened to people?

I didn't think of the ending,

What happened to our time?

Masculine is a feminine quality,

Women know their own men.

It's all crazy,

What happened to our time?

Sometimes I think,

Don't wake up if you have a dream.

Am I oblivious or am I

What happened to our time?

Our grandfather Temur is our descendants

Our human disciples are like Navoi.

After all, we are the future generations

What happened to our time?

Immoral people are increasing,

He is a human being, apes.

Money is a stupid animal

What happened to our time?

Shame, there is no honor left,

No one knows yet, right?

You can't live with shame

What happened to our time?

Respect for the elder is honor for the younger

Now respect for money, respect for career

Is there any wisdom in this

What is wrong with our time?

I got excited thinking about these things

I couldn't find the answer after searching

I say again and again crying

What is wrong with our time?

6
Calling Navoi

Mir Alisher Navoi is our great grandfather

Our world-recognized Turkic grandfather

He was the Sultan of Ghazal estate

Our grandfather can live forever

No one can replace him

Nobody can be like Navoi

"Yesterday" is always in our hearts

No one can write a ghazal like him.

Hossein was a friend of Boygaro

Always burned for the people

He is passionate about poetry

Grandfather Lutfi even admired it.

Such a person comes into the world

everyone is equally dear

Grandfather Navoi, who has a place in my heart

is dear every moment.

Reading your ghazals increases my love

Our grandfather starts everyone to be good.

He still lives in our hearts

Those who miss Navoi have youth in their eyes

7
Faithful

Temperance at all times

Never knowing Hadding

Will you come to the motherland?

Make you info from your hand.

Feelings are a fleeting illusion

Don't believe in wealth

There is no loyalty in the beautiful

Don't worry about Hijran.

Get rid of your career

Get out of the way if your friends beat you

Be faithful to God

Repent sincerely

A mother is a friend and supporter

Faithful is the faithful

Be loyal to those who are loyal

This world itself is transitory.

What will be left of us in the world

Be loyal to the country.

Our children are behind us

Don't do it sometimes.

8
The future of Uzbekistan

We study, we search

We strive for a new life.

Our country is our future

We are proud of it.

Uzbekistan has a great future

Our country is a paradise

Our country is a garden

A place for loving hearts.

The honor of our country is in the sky

The power is in the youth

A bar of enthusiasm

In eager volunteer hearts.

Surkhanim has a price

He has a stake in the future of Uzbekistan.

The future of our country is in the youth

Our future is in safe hands.

Uzbekistan has a great past

Our Motherland recognized by the world

The future of Uzbekistan is great

We honor OUR COUNTRY.

The future of Uzbekistan is in chess players

The future of Uzbekistan is in the wrestlers

Boxers are the future of Uzbekistan

The future of Uzbekistan is in athletes.

Leading in every field,

Our country is rising

The future of Uzbekistan is great

Our country is alive

The future of Uzbekistan is in our hands

God bless us on our way

As Muslims, the Qur'an is in our hearts

Islam is our greatness.

9
People have changed

People have no love left

There is a lot of anger in his eyes

No one has patience left

What they do is only suffering.

The people I know have changed

Maybe they are much older

He gave up on regret

Kindness has forgotten love

I respect you endlessly

you don't remember

Wealth is without feeling

Can a person be heartless?

I was heartbroken to see you

My dreams were distracted, broken.

My eyes filled with tears

People's dream was broken because of money.

10
My phone

I can't leave you, my phone
I have no life without you.
Be with me every moment, always
The essence of my life, my love.

Imo, WhatsApp, Telegram, Instagram
I am in all of them
If the money goes away, the wife also goes away
No antenna, not working internet

Then disaster will befall me
A huge burden is crushing my heart
You can live without love and sleep
Some people can't live without a phone like me.

Google and YouTube show the world
Find any information in it
How many sessions the phone closes
The joke is that this poem can live without a phone

11
You don't love me

I miss you in my heart

My precious soul

You live in my dreams

My eyes are on your ways, my soul

Sorry, my love, you don't know

You don't even look at me

It's a pity that life is this life, my dear

I have no more left to live

I live with hope

One day I will reach you

My beautiful dreams are with you

One day you will come to me before I sleep.

I live with hope

One day I will reach you

My beautiful dreams are with you

One day you will come to me before I sleep.

Wherever you are, you are in my heart

One day you will miss me crazy

You don't know my heartache

Too bad you don't love me

12
Good luck

Your presence in this life is happiness

It is happiness to pass the tests of God

It is happiness to receive blessings by serving

It is a blessing to have a family in your destiny.

Don't be fooled by any lies

Don't fall into sin and gossip

Do not suffer in this life

Don't get tired of smiles

The beauty of your beautiful face

I wish you good health always

May your eyes be meaningful

Let us divide like flowers

Do not let dreams go to you

Don't let suffering settle in your heart

Don't let the madman fall into his trap

Do not let regret accompany you

Bakhtigul listen to my word to you

I will remind you that in a hurry life

You will achieve what God has called you

Be honest and you will be happy, trust me.

13
Happy day

The moments we have been waiting for have come
Happiness came to us
Our dreams have begun
My heart started pounding

We've had trouble on this road
Coordinating pain and suffering
Only striving for our happiness
We endured with patience

Today is our wedding day
Let every moment be filled with happiness
Step into a new life
The moment when we can feel happiness.

Friends are laughing happily around
We spend the night in the sound of cheering
Our parents pray for happiness
We have all been waiting for this day

This day is a gift of fate
The owner of my heart is with me today
I will remember this day
Today is the happiest day of my life...

14
To the tourist

Sayyodkhan is a beautiful traveler

who does not have a grudge in his heart

The name he chose for himself is Hayat Khan

A cook, open hearted, kind

Happiness, beloved friend Farkhondjon.

Beloved daughter-in-law of his mother-in-law

You can do your service and find your heart

Don't hurt anyone's tongue

He always does his work with love

Yasmina Khan's sister, she is the best

His mother's firstborn, beloved, husband

His eyes are bright with happiness

A beautiful mistress of a happy household

His jokes are heartwarming

Arzla has young eyes

Throw stones at him

Don't let the tears flow from your eyes

Sayyod Khan, who went to Olsilar

Sayyodkhan who achieved his dreams

Sayyodkhan withstood the tests

I wrote this poem for you Sayyodkhan

15
Memories

I remembered you back in the past

I cried a little while looking at your picture

How many promises are left

I forget when I didn't know you.

I remember with sadness

You left me in the distance

You walk and live drunk with happiness

I'm not living with others.

Is it easy to forget love?

Destroying the human heart is the end

My heart is suffering from life

I'm human too, after all.

I was happy in the garden of love

The moments that remain in my memories

When it becomes irreversible

Why I couldn't forget him.

I couldn't find love anywhere else

He is still alone in my heart

Love lives in my memories

It is impossible to reach it only.

16
Winter

Winter has arrived

It finally snowed.

The days got colder too

The surroundings are also very cold.

The birds also flew away

He reached the hot places.

The first snow fell

Nature took on a different color.

A soft snowflake is falling

The fir tree in our yard was covered with white snow.

A beautiful snowflake is falling

The snowflake we long missed.

The days we miss have come

There is little time left for the new year.

The blizzard game has also started

Our hearts were delighted.

17
Life

Have you tried life?

Don't you feel tired life?

Don't get tired of tormenting me, life

Are you happy to see my condition, life?

I was deceived into believing that they said I love them

I didn't know what was in my dress.

I did not understand why I came into the world

I did not know how to live

I can't find a cure for my pain

I can't live with this pain

I can't find my place in life

I can't deal with this pain anymore

My heart is crying, I have no choice

I have no support in my heart.

Poor me, I don't know why

Oh life, I don't trust anyone.

I'm crazy, I'm crazy, I'm crazy
I don't know happiness, my heart is full of joy.
I really loved you
But I can't find a cure for my pain.

I need this life
Salvation after I couldn't find it
Sivdim, you did not love me life
You just broke my heart.

I'm used to being alone
To myself - I complain about life.
Don't believe in tomorrow - believe
Believing in happiness is unfortunate.

I'm worthless to anyone
Whom I despise too much
It is a pleasure to whom I despise
Do you need life?

Since death is transitory,

Life itself is really short.

Someone is happy, someone is unhappy

Life is a never-ending trial

18
Boring life

I'm bored of the silences of life

I'm tired of life's trials.

I left my dreams

I am satisfied with the stems of life.

I did not know what happiness is

Don't ask what happiness is

I don't know what life is

Don't ask what life is

Whatever I do, it's the opposite

Like my unfulfilled dream.

Eh, why is life like this?

Like my other unanswered questions.

19
My mom

I'm not worth the tears my mother shed

If I cry, I don't like my mother.

Give me a chance to live, I'll make my mother happy,

I don't ask you anything but life.

My support, my support, my only mother,

My teacher, my friend, my prayer mother.

I don't need life without you, mom

My love, dear mother.

20
Truth

I could not find the truth in life

I looked for him all the way

Where are you hiding?

Ask who you are

I couldn't find it, I'm tired of looking

I'm looking for a way to go

If I could find it, I would bring it

Some would cry

The truth is that I can't find you

Please let me know

It's crashing because you're not there

There are so many sprouts

You hide, tell me how much more

Don't you feel sorry for the injustice?

What is the price of the sold conscience

I would have paid if you had come

Why are you silent when you need it?

Why don't you show up at the right time?

He said that he will go if you are available

Why not when you are waiting

Sorry, I'm tired of waiting

But I haven't seen you yet

I don't know how to live anymore

The truth is, I couldn't find you.

21
My meaningless days

I lived waiting for tomorrow

I believed, waiting for tomorrow

I lived waiting for tomorrow

Forgetting the sufferings of yesterday

What now? What can I do now?

I say that my day is over

I don't know how to live

What now? I don't know what I'm waiting for

They say yesterday is the past

I can't remember the memories

They say tomorrow is the future

That's all I've lost faith in

Today is the only day in my life

Today I live thinking that it is over

Both yesterday and tomorrow to me today

I'm sorry today is a meaningless day

When the dark nights will end

When the sun shines

When will the cloudy days end?

When will my meaningful days come?

22
Love

You come once in life

You love, you are loved

One day you will be happy

You forget your pains

You call it love

You love love

You hurt your loved one

You know your worth when you don't have it

You burn because of love

You touch the ground if you don't love

You will regret it

You will be happy with your lover

You will be there in an instant

You dream about him

Do not rush, you will reach him one day

23
Depression

Life gives you such pain

Chidarkansan got used to it all

You will neither live nor live in life

You only feel sorry for the past life

When your friend becomes your enemy

Believe me, your heart will break

Your life is full of trials

There will be more than you expect

It is a test to be given wealth and a position

Everything is a life choice given to us

Can someone help me if I fall?

When life gives you a test

I am with you, I take your pains

I am your support, I will be your support

I love you very much

He says that only my mother knows these things

When I'm depressed

On my head when disaster strikes

Only my mother was with me

The rest left a pain in my heart

When I was a child, my dreams were the sky

It's just a dream

I suddenly thought

A moment of depression

I can't come to myself

To my regretted life

I feel sorry for myself

The sale was heavy on my head

One day these days

One day bright days will come

Gone are the days of despair

I have dark nights in my head now.

www.ingramcontent.com/pod-product-compliance
Lightning Source LLC
LaVergne TN
LVHW010417070526
838199LV00064B/5324